W9-CTV-997

Peary Caribou

by Grace Hansen

Abdo Kids Jumbo is an Imprint of Abdo Kids
abdobooks.com

abdobooks.com

Published by Abdo Kids, a division of ABDO, P.O. Box 398166, Minneapolis, Minnesota 55439.
Copyright © 2020 by Abdo Consulting Group, Inc. International copyrights reserved in all countries.
No part of this book may be reproduced in any form without written permission from the publisher.
Abdo Kids Jumbo™ is a trademark and logo of Abdo Kids.

Printed in the United States of America, North Mankato, Minnesota.

102019

012020

THIS BOOK CONTAINS
RECYCLED MATERIALS

Photo Credits: Alamy, iStock, Minden Pictures, National Geographic Image Collection, Shutterstock

Production Contributors: Teddy Borth, Jennie Forsberg, Grace Hansen
Design Contributors: Dorothy Toth, Pakou Moua

Library of Congress Control Number: 2019941226
Publisher's Cataloging-in-Publication Data

Names: Hansen, Grace, author.

Title: Peary caribou / by Grace Hansen

Description: Minneapolis, Minnesota : Abdo Kids, 2020 | Series: Arctic animals | Includes online
    resources and index.

Identifiers: ISBN 9781532188886 (lib. bdg.) | ISBN 9781532189371 (ebook) | ISBN 9781098200350
    (Read-to-Me ebook)

Subjects: LCSH: Peary caribou--Juvenile literature. | Caribou--Juvenile literature. | Zoology--Arctic
    regions--Juvenile literature. | Arctic--Juvenile literature.

Classification: DDC 599.73--dc23

Table of Contents

The Arctic

The Arctic is the northernmost part of Earth. It is made up of land, the Arctic Ocean, and the **sea ice** that floats on it. The weather there is freezing cold. Any animal that lives in the Arctic is tough!

4

Peary Caribou

Peary caribou are the smallest and lightest caribou species. However, they still are able to survive in the harshest places.

6

Their very **dense** coats keep them warm. Their coats are mostly white in color in the wintertime. In summer, their coats are shorter and darker.

Peary caribou have shorter **muzzles** than other caribou **species**. They also have short, furry ears. These things help keep in heat.

10

These caribou have large feet and hooves. They can easily walk over snow and ice.

Their **hooves** also help the caribou dig for food. In the wintertime, their food is covered in snow. They have to dig for the dried grasses.

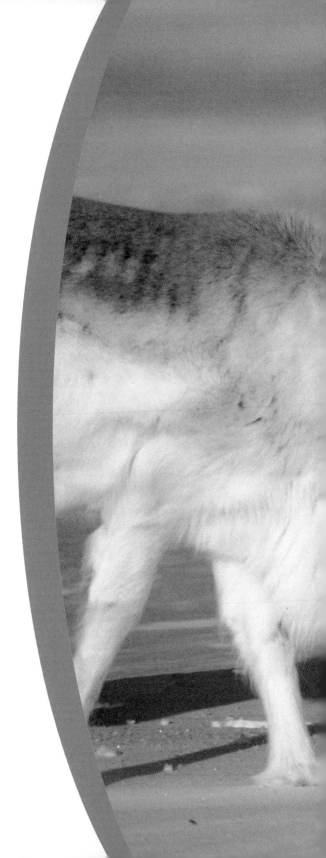

Peary Caribou move seasonally. They are always searching for food. In the summer, their favorite plant to eat is purple saxifrage. It stains their **muzzles**!

16

purple saxifrage

17

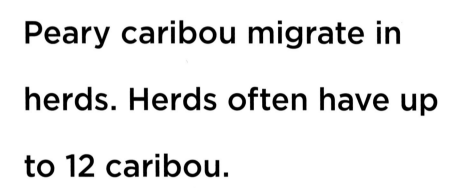

Peary caribou migrate in herds. Herds often have up to 12 caribou.

19

Baby Peary Caribou

Females are able to have babies if they get enough to eat in the summer. Calves are born the next June. Herds grow larger in summer to help protect the new calves.

21

More Facts

- Peary caribou can live for at least 15 years in the wild.

- Peary caribou got their name from Robert Peary. He was an American explorer who was born in Cresson, Pennsylvania, in 1856. He began exploring the Arctic in 1886.

- The Canadian Arctic is the only place where Peary caribou live.

Glossary

dense – having parts very close together with little space between.

harsh – very rough and not pleasing.

hoof – the hard, tough covering on the feet of certain mammals.

muzzle – the part of the head of some animals that contains the nose, jaws, and mouth.

sea ice – frozen ocean water that is typically covered with snow.

species – a group of living things that look alike and can have offspring together.

23

Index

Abdo Kids
ONLINE
FREE! ONLINE MULTIMEDIA RESOURCES

Visit **abdokids.com** to access crafts, games, videos, and more!

Use Abdo Kids code

APK8886

or scan this QR code!